CW00448806

Spirit Sister Dance

Norbert Krapf

Fernwood
PRESS

Spirit Sister Dance

©2022 by Norbert Krapf

Fernwood Press
Newberg, Oregon
www.fernwoodpress.com

All rights reserved. No part may be reproduced
for any commercial purpose by any method without
permission in writing from the copyright holder.

Printed in the United States of America

Cover and page design: Mareesa Fawver Moss

Cover photo: Liza Hyatt

Author photo: © Andreas Riedel

ISBN 978-1-59498-090-9

in honor of Marilyn,
my spirit sister

and for Mary,
my earth sister
now become spirit

Contents

Acknowledgments

Some of these poems originally appeared in the Bellevue Press Postcard Series ("Sisters"), *Flying Island* ("Stillborn Love Song"), *Poetrybay* ("Sister Song"), *Valparaiso Poetry Review* ("Still Dark"), and the Airpoets' anthology *Rivers, Rails, and Runways* (San Francisco Bay Press, 2008): "Angel Sister Song."

"Sister Query" and "Sister Song" were included in *Bloodroot: Indiana Poems* (Indiana University Press, 2008) and are reprinted by permission of the publisher, and a small selection of the poems, for which the author holds all rights, appeared in *Sweet Sister Moon* (WordTech Editions, 2009, now o.p.).

Thanks to the editors of these publications for giving these poems an earlier home and for permission to reprint, and especially to Liza Hyatt for her suggestions.

Acknowledgments

Some of these poems originally appeared in the Bellevue Press Poetry editions ("Sister"), Fitting Home ("Stillborn Lover Song," "Freedman ("Sister Song") "California Poetry Review ("Still Drill"), and the Aspens Anthology; Parts, Park, and Bread ("San Francisco Bay Press, 2008). Vegetable Song ("Sister Opera" and "Siren Song") were included in Blue Front Indiana Poems (Indiana University Press, 2008) and are reprinted by permission of the publisher, and a small selection of the poems, for which the author holds all rights, appeared in Word Star Moon (Word Tech Editions 2009, now op.).

Thanks to the editors of these publications for giving these poems an earlier home and for permission to reprint, and especially to Lisa Head for her suggestions.

We think by feeling. What is there to know?
I hear my being dance from ear to ear.
I wake to sleep, and take my waking slow.

—Theodore Roethke, "The Waking"

Where is my core?
What inwardnesses are
Unseen, unsounded?

—Ursula K. Le Guin, "Outsight"

Dance is the hidden language of the soul.

—Martha Graham

We think by feeling. What is there to know?
I hear my being dance from ear to ear.
I wake to sleep, and take my waking slow.

—Theodore Roethke, "The Waking"

Where is my core?
What inward selves are
Linear unsounded?

—Ursula K. Le Guin, "Outsight"

Dance is the hidden language of the soul

—Martha Graham

Sisters

My first sister
was born without
ever drawing a
breath. I heard
my mother cry
and my grandmother
scold her upstairs.

* * *

When my second sister
began to cry,
my mother breathed
a lot easier. My
grandmother smiled.
The dolls we kept
clapped their hands.

Sisters

My little sister
was born without
ever drawing a
breath. I heard
my mother cry
and my grandmother
scold her parents.

When my second sister
began to cry
my mother brushed
a lot each. My
grandmother smiled
The cloth we kept
slapped their hands.

Song for a Sister

Back at the site of your tiny tomb,
Sister, still not sure what to say.

First fact: Born Jan. 25, 1950.
Second fact: Died Jan. 25, 1950.
This year you would
have turned forty-five.

They named you Marilyn,
but you may have been gone
by the time the name was given.
Or perhaps the name was selected
and waiting like a baptismal
gown sewn for you to fit into.

I don't know whether to say
you died in being born
or were already dead
before you could be born.

I never saw you.
I miss you more
for never having seen you,
and I believe in you.

Whenever I return from
the island in the East,
I come back to your small
stone on which it is carved:
GONE TO BE AN ANGEL.

Halcyon times, the time
of your birth and death,
the pundits tell us,
but I remember our mother's
grief all too well, the sound
of her sobs descending the stairs
from the bedroom in which
her mother scolded her hard.

Grandma's husband, you may know,
left her and this world at age thirty-three
with six young children on the farm.
No time for self-pity. Pigs to feed
and butcher. Meals to cook,
clothes to wash, crops to put in.

Our father swallowed his grief
over the loss of a daughter,
carried it for years.
It had to tear at his guts.

Marilyn, when I talk to you,
I speak to that part of myself
I have not been lucky enough
to discover but which will one
day rejoin and complete me.

The green grass of summer
grows around your clean-carved,
well-trimmed tombstone
not far from the tall tomb
of the maternal ancestor
who came from Lohr am Main.

To return here
from far away
and try to preserve
even the slightest trace
of you is to pay
tribute to a life so dear,
its mysterious end
arrived as it began.

Sister Query

How does it feel, Sister, to die
as you are born? Surely you were
alive in our mother's womb?

Did you never draw one breath
in this or any other world?
Am I the single believer in this

religion of one, with you as
center and source of my creed?
Are all those I love in this realm

doubting Thomases when it comes
to you and your invisible life?
Is it your breath I hear

and sometimes feel in the night
when everyone else sleeps?
Will I one day wake to look

into your soulful eyes that have
looked at me across this divide
since I was born? Could I have

been stillborn in this realm apart
from you and those who left here
to join with you? Will I one day

see the light in your eyes wherever
they went before they could open
and walk with you however

you have walked since the day
you were born and died in and out
of whatever world is still mine?

Sister Song

Oh, Sister,
when you came
into and left this
world without
ever drawing
a breath, I felt
a tremor
in the house,
and sadness hung
for years like
smoke beneath
the kitchen ceiling
until another sister
came and stayed

and ever since
that day of
your birth and death,
I have felt around
the world like
a blind brother
to touch you
and bring you back.

Angel Sister Song

1.

Marilyn, Marilyn,
I say your name to summon
you back into this world
they say you never were in.
Those who see it so are
unborn into your presence.

2.

Born dead, born still,
means you always
were spirit, my sister.
Never flesh, always spirit,
born still, you live
for me outside time,
my sister stillborn.

3.

Speak, Sister, speak.
For decades I've been
training these ears to hear
the voice of an angel
who never found a home
in flesh. Sing, Sister,
sing in spirit breath.

4.

Teach me, Marilyn,
to sing a song that will
wing me into your world
that waits beyond
the one in which I live.
Angel Sister, breathe
spirit song into my ear.

Still Dark

It is still dark
when I rise
in the town

where I was born
but have not lived
for sixty years

and dress
and follow my
feet to the large

sandstone church
and the open gate
into the old cemetery

to the crucifix marking
the grave of the
Croatian missionary

priest who brought
German Catholics
into these hills

a hundred years
before you and I
were conceived;

past the tombstone
carved in German
script honoring

the ancestor who died
only three years after he
and his wife and their

six *Kinder* arrived;
veer slightly to
the left as a hint

of gray appears
over my head;
stop at the third

row of tiny tombstones
and move into
the damp grass

to find the small
granite stone fourth
in from the lane;

and wait for light
to find your name,
Marilyn Krapf,

daughter of Dorothy
and Clarence,
and the lettering,

carved to endure,
of the single date
that tells the story

and confirms
the mystery
of your birth

that I can never
stop reflecting on
no matter how

many times I
come back to
our hometown.

The Sister in the Circle

If there is a circle,
will it still be unbroken
when I come inside?

Are you still waiting,
my sister stillborn,
inside the circle?

Are you connected
inside the circle
to Mother and Father?

Will the circle inside
of which we come together
be unbroken for all time?

Has it been you I've been
hearing all these years singing
for me to come home?

After End Time

I have projected your life
into end time because it

ended when it began,
from one point of view.

But from another, what
is the beginning, and what

is the end? And how do
they differ, and how much

distance or space is there
in between and where?

And for how long
and how do the rest

of us live? And how
deep are our lives?

And how far down
do they go into

the realm of spirit?
And how would we

measure our spirit life
in terms of seconds, minutes,

years, and the passage of time
and non-time or being outside

of time? What would be
the standard of progress

and growth of the life
lived only in the dimension

of the spiritual, Spirit Sister?
What will you have to say

to me, your brother, Marilyn,
when I enter end time?

Breath from the Other Side

I saw breath on the other side
of the window but heard
not one syllable of sound.

This breath left a kind of print
but not one made by a foot.
It was more like a hieroglyph.

I knew I could not yet speak
that language, but a part
of me could intuit bits.

What the breath print said
was to be patient, one day
you will come to understand.

Sometimes the issue is not
learning how to speak a language
but to grasp who speaks it.

I don't know how long I stared
at this snowflake of frozen breath,
but at some point I recognized

the spirit of the one who had
left this unique print for me.
She knew I would look for as

long as it would take me
to absorb the message she left:
I am the sister you once thought

you lost. But here I am, on the other
side of this window, waiting for you.
Don't worry. I can wait forever.

Dream Catcher

I want to be your dream catcher,
Spirit Sister. I want to catch

the dream I have had of you
and release it into the winds

and the rays of the sun that
shine on raindrops that fall

holding luminous images of you.
Your life dream is more real

to me than the news reports
of things that happen every day.

To catch the dream that
I have had of you, Sister,

does not mean I want to trap you,
but catch you and release you

for others to see and hear
the song of your wings as they

climb beyond the here and now.
May this poem be the dream catcher

that holds you alive in my
memory and allows you to

inspire others to spirit dream
about the world you're in.

Invisible Gift

Sister, I send you
a gift for those no
longer allowed to
breathe in this world.

I send you one
breath of human love
from a brother left
behind in this world.

Marilyn is your name.
Mary Lou is your sister.
Norbert, Edgar, and Leonard
are your brothers.

I would have us here
breathe together toward
you in a spiritual Morse
code of those still living

in our world to say
that your breath from
yours comes to us
into ours as love.

The Right Touch

Part of you must have remained
beyond so close to me that

I did not have the eyes to
perceive the shape you took.

Sometimes I did think I heard
someone breathe in my bedroom.

Sometimes I thought I heard
a soft footstep on a floorboard.

Once or twice reading in bed
I did hear an ancient song

coming to me out of the air.
Was that you, Spirit Sister?

Maybe if I had reached out in
the right way, I'd have touched you.

But having the right kind of touch
can take an infinity to develop.

Tuning My Ears

Sister, Sister, I envision you
there with Mother and Father.

You are as evanescent as a cloud
but as pure as the first snowflake.

When the sunlight shines through
you from behind, you glow like

the petals of a flower suffused
with the light of the gods.

How tender the sound of
your spirit breath. How silken

the strands of your angel hair
I am not able to touch.

Sing to me in that soft voice
both familiar and ethereal.

You may be surprised at how well
my ears are attuned to your pitch.

Tuning My Ears

Sister, Sister, I envision you
there with Mother and Father.

You are as evanescent as a cloud
but as pure as the first snowflake.

When the sunlight shines through
you from behind, you glow like

the petals of a flower suffused
with the light of the gods.

How tender the sound of
your soft breath. How silken

the strands of your angel hair
I am not able to touch.

Sing to me in that soft voice
both familiar and ethereal.

You may be surprised at how well
my ears are attuned to your pitch.

Dancing with the Invisible

It feels good to do this dance
with the invisible. Do I know

where to take my next step?
Not always, but when I close

my eyes, my feet know
where they want to go.

Once the eyes see in the dark,
a light not visible before remains.

Have you danced with an angel?
I did, and she is my sister.

When she puts out her spirit hand,
I take it and go where she leads,

which is where I have never been
but have always wanted to go.

So I follow where she leads. My
feet grow light and deft when

I am so lucky and blessed
as to dance with a spirit sister.

The rhythm you feel as you read
these lines comes from her.

Queries for Marilyn

Why is spirit
so often bigger

than any religion?
Why can't we

on this side
see you over

there on that side
better than we do?

The farther I get
from your sad birth

the better I see
into the world

where you live
outside time.

One of these days
my time will stop

and I'll no longer
be blind to you.

The Division

Seventy years ago, one
winter, a baby girl came

and left at the same
time. Some years

later another baby
sister came, and we

heard her cry
and rejoiced.

Now I know you came
again into my second sister,

whom I love. But she too
has left this world before me.

You two are now one spirit
divided into two, two halves

of a love that I see as ever
growing more beautiful.

The Division

Seventy years ago one
winter a baby girl came

and left at the same
time. Some years

later another baby
sister came, and we

heard her cry
and rejoiced.

Now I know you came
again into my second sister

whom I love. But she too
has left this world before me.

You two are now one spirit
divided into two halves

of a love that I see as ever
growing more beautiful.

Spiritual Recovery

Something I must tell you
that you may already know,

Marilyn: When some readers
hear or read what I say to

or about you, they tell me
they are sorry for my loss.

I become confused. I am
grateful for their compassion

and concern, but I say
to myself, *This is not loss.*

This is a great recovery.
To think about you, to talk

to you, to know I am
coming closer and closer

to joining you and becoming
one with you, one with myself,

one in spirit with the angel
that lives within me, is

nothing but a blessing. No
thing could be more beautiful.

Where Were You?

Were you in the rain
that splattered on the roof
and beaded on the windows
as if asking to come in?

Were you in the snowflakes
that settled on brown grass
and gradually turned it white
and then accepted our
footprints as we trudged
through you after white
deepened and we cupped
and shaped you into balls
we lobbed at one another?

Were you in the wind
that lifted the dust
and swirled it across the rock
road toward the house
and lifted the leaves
on the pin oaks in the front
yard and bent and roughed up
the branches that eventually
stopped moving and settled?

Were you in the warm water
of the ponds in which we dropped
our hooks baited with worms?

Were you inside the tomatoes
that grew on the vines
of the plants we stuck
in the earth in the garden
after the seeds germinated
and green leaves came out?

Were you in the rays
of sunlight that slanted
onto our skin and turned
us brown in the summer,
making us feel healthy?

Were you in the earth
that our bare summer feet
touched over and over
as we played to our
hearts' content before
school started again?

Were you inside of us
to come out in the breath
we exhaled and the words
and other sounds that
came out of our mouths?

Were you in the sleep,
which stuck to the corners
of our eyes, we rubbed away
as we woke up in the morning?

Were you inside the tears
our mother cried when we
knelt around the bed
praying the rosary
before our second sister
came into our world
and made us smile?

Were you inside the tears
that escaped from our
father's eyes after he
came back home from
the hospital where they
sent electricity through
his body to calm his nerves?

What You Were

You were the song
I wanted to sing
but did not know
how to bring forth.

You were the poem
ripening to come forth
until I learned how
to let you loose.

You were the prayer
on my tongue
that I did not
know how to turn
in the right way
to release you.

You were the spirit
waiting to speak
until I found
a way to open
both of my ears.

You were the guardian
that looked out for me
when I thought I knew
how to take care of myself.

So Patient

So many years I didn't
think about you when I
went away and made
my way into the world.

So many things I did
without realizing
you were a part of them.

So many thoughts I had
without understanding
that you were at
the edge of them.

So long you waited,
so patient you were,
so deep was the love
you kept giving me

until I woke up
to your invisible presence
that came with me
wherever I went.

Blessed Be the Sister

Blessed be the sister
who did not whimper
about being left behind
beneath the tiny tombstone,
waiting to be revisited

because she knew
she was with me
all the while I inched
toward an awakening
to her presence in me.

Blessed be the sister
traveling so light
and so very quiet
as she came with me.

Blessed be the sister
for the spirit
she gave to me
even though I may
not have known
how much it
was a part of me.

Blessed be her spirit
for growing larger
and stronger in me.

The Mystery Sister

Marilyn, you are a mystery
flashing in and out of history.

You are a blue eye
opening in the sky.

Everywhere I look,
I read you in my book.

When you came, you also went.
Were you a message God sent?

They told me you were born still.
I pray I see you over the next hill.

You are spirit invisible,
from us siblings indivisible.

You touch me in a way
no human voice could say.

Little Girls Lost and Found

Speak to me, Mother.
Speak to me from beyond.
Tell me of the little girl
you lost. I knew,
I knew why you cried
ever so quietly. I had
no words to say to you,
but I was all ears.

You lost one little
girl, and you sobbed,
Mother, but you found
another little girl, didn't
you, and then smiled.

I remember those years
when you sobbed.
They were not many,
but they must have seemed
long because of your little
girl lost. But, oh, Mother,
there was also little girl found.

Know what, my sad
mother? Your little
girl found told me
she wished you had
told her more about
your little girl lost.
Mary wanted to hear
more about Marilyn.

I am doing my best
to tell my part
of the story, so little
girl found meets little
girl lost. I love them
both, Mother—they
came from you.

Know what I know,
Mother, who sobbed
and who smiled?
Your little girl lost
is my little girl found.
Somewhere along the way,
I found your little girl
lost and let her speak.
I let her speak to me.

Do you remember when
you let me hold your
little girl found? When
I held your little girl
found, your new baby
girl, a part of me knew
I was also holding
your little girl lost.

My little sister lost was
also my little sister found.
Little girl lost came
inside little girl found.
Little sister found,
I hereby give you
little sister lost.

Little Girl Lost Blues

Brother wants to sing you something low down and blue.
Sis, he wants to sing you something low down and blue.
You got to know it all comes back to losing you.

Should he sing you "Baby Please Don't Go"?
Do you want to hear "Baby Please Don't Go"?
Answer's got to be why no, Brother, no!

Brother, tell me I ain't been gone now seventy years.
Brother, how could it be I been gone seventy years?
Since I was born and died, no, no, not seventy years!

The good news, Sis, is that what's lost can be found.
The good news, Sis, is you were lost but now are found.
Now that brother found you, he can see you all around.

Sister's in the sky and the land and the sea.
Sister's in the sky and the land and the sea.
Sister's spirit lives right here inside me.

Where You Live

I just can't stop writing about you.
Some might think you've always been
only a figment of my imagination

but living in someone's imagination
does not mean you never lived.
If we live only as spirit,

does that make us dead to the world?
If we live only within a poem
or within someone's memory

does that mean we never live
in the here or in the now?
Did we always live outside time

if we never lived inside the flesh?
What if we always lived in spirit?
What if we always transcended time?

Maybe you always lived beyond.
Maybe you always lived above.
Maybe you always lived within.

Maybe you're the spirit inside my skin.
Maybe you're the spirit in my blood.
Maybe you're the vision in my eye.

Little Flame

Could you who never
cried be the song
I hear inside?

Are you the song
I hear but can't sing
with my voice?

The sweet spirit
that hovers just
beyond my words?

The pure vision
flickering just
beyond my eyes?

The flame we
see on the wick
in the storm?

The point of
light we see
in the dark?

The air that
comes in
and goes out

when we sleep
and wake
once again?

When I Grow Up

I want to be
the words that
speak your language,

the translator
who ferries you
over from spirit

to flesh but allows
you to remain
in the original.

I want to speak
your language
of spirit.

Be the voice
that sings your
gospel tune.

The soul
that is one
with you.

When I Grow Up

I want to be
the words that
speak your language

the translator
who ferries you
over from spirit

to flesh but allows
you to remain
in the original

I want to speak
your language
of spirit

Be the voice
that sings your
gospel tune

The soul
that is one
with you.

The Hand in Mine

We are lying side by side,
my stillborn sister and I.

We are both looking up.
We need not say anything.

We lie together for a long time
before I realize her hand

has found its way into mine.
It's not easy to know

when a spirit hand has
slipped its way into yours

because the touch is so delicate.
There is a slight tingle

as quiet as a touch can be.
I know why she is here.

She is my female other half.
She is my spirit other half.

Together we make one whole.
She has come to lead me

back home to the other side.
That's why her hand is in mine.

It is dark outside, but when
the sun begins to rise,

we will walk away together.
I see she has been waiting.

Overheard Solos

I think you would have played
the violin. I can see you tuck

it under your chin. I love
the way you hold the bow,

so delicate, but also with
command. Your vibrato is pure

and almost ethereal, as if you
were born into this world

and the next one at the same
time. The music you make,

my sister who lives in two
worlds, is all double-stops,

all in cut time, and goes where
most notes never dare ascend.

Such purity of tone sets you
worlds apart. How I listen!

What I can hear! Your bow
leads me across strings I never

imagined I could cross, toward
a country I never envisioned.

Stillborn Love Song

I love you when
the dusk thickens,
evening falls in every
direction, and the dove
coos ever more forlorn.

I love you when
October air turns crisp
and smoke rises like
the breath of angels
from the chimneys.

I love you, Soul Sister,
when everything turns so quiet
the only sound I think I hear
is the settling of snowflakes
on branches above my head.

I love you most when
All Souls' Day returns
and the veil between
your world and mine lifts

and your spirit breath
drifts back down to earth
and touches these lips
waiting for your spirit kiss.

Still in the House

I am still in the house
at 415 East 15th Street
in Jasper, Indiana.

It is still midwinter,
and we are sad because
you have been born,

but somebody forgot
to let you cry so we could
know you are with us.

But this is the kind
of sadness families
and individuals keep

to themselves until someone
acknowledges they too share
such a loss in their family.

These poems of and for you,
Sister Marilyn, are my way
of opening a small door

through which others
may step, however quietly,
to come together and build

a community, however
small its circle, that
grows in spirit

as our stories go around,
and others can listen
and more may speak.

Still Being Born

It comes to me that
your eyes are the pale
blue of our father's.

I can also see that
your hair is the strawberry
blonde of our sister Mary's.
She got hers from our
father's mother, Mary.

And I can hear now
that your voice has
the pitch and timbre
of our mother Dorothy's
when she would sing
the Tennessee Waltz.

Maybe you were the darling
she was always dancing with.

For sure, it is yours,
a voice I hear in mine
when I try to sing
the song my entire life
has been writing.

Marilyn, you are the song
I am writing and singing.

You are the voice
that will make me whole.
You are the rebirth
I am preparing to have.

Continuing the Dance

Marilyn, you are teaching
me how to dance.

I am learning how
to take spirit steps.

I don't care if anybody
else hears this music

to which you and I
do our special dance.

People think I am
dancing by myself.

But how lucky I am
to have this chance!

I love your delicate step,
how you take the lead.

My sister, my beautiful
soul sister, you came back

to listen and dance me
into your spirit world.

I savor the delicate
whisper of your voice,

the deft movement
of your leading feet.

Continuing the Dance

Marilyn, you are teaching
me how to dance.

I am learning how
to take spins steps.

I don't care if anybody
else hears this music

to which you and I
do our special dance.

People think I am
dancing by myself.

But how lucky I am
to have this chance.

I love your different step,
how you take the lead.

My sister, my beautiful
soul sister, you came back

to listen and dance me
into your quiet world.

I savor the delicate
whisper of your voice.

the deft movement
of your leading feet.

About the Author

Norbert Krapf, a native of Jasper, Indiana, is a former Indiana Poet Laureate. For thirty-four years, he taught at Long Island University while directing the C.W. Post Poetry Center for eighteen of those years. In 2004, he retired and moved with his family to Indianapolis. He taught American poetry as a Fulbright Fellow at the University of Freiburg (1980-81) and the University of Erlangen-Nuremberg (1988-89). His previous books include fourteen poetry collections such as *Somewhere in Southern Indiana* (1993), *Looking for God's Country* (2005), *Bloodroot: Indiana Poems* (2008), *Sweet Sister Moon* (2009), *Songs in Sepia and Black and White* (2012), *Catholic Boy Blues* (2015), *Indiana Hill Country Poems* (2019), and *Southwest by Midwest* (2020). Garrison Keillor has read his poems on *The Writer's Almanac,* and he has a poem in stained glass at the Indianapolis International Airport.

Krapf is the author of four volumes of prose memoirs: *The Ripest Moments: A Southern Indiana Childhood* (2008), the experimental *American Dreams: Reveries and Revisitations* (2013), *Shrinking the Monster: Healing the Wounds of Our Abuse* (2016), and the forthcoming *Homecomings: A Writer's Memoir* (2023), which covers the fifty years of his writing and publishing life. He has collaborated with Indiana photographers Darryl Jones, David Pierini, and Richard Fields, and German photographer

Andreas Riedel. With pianist-composer Monika Herzig, he released the jazz and poetry CD *Imagine* (2017), and he performs poetry and blues with Indiana bluesman Gordon Bonham. He has received the Lucille Medwick Memorial Award from the Poetry Society of America, a Creative Renewal Fellowship from the Arts Council of Indianapolis, and a Glick Indiana Author Award. It is no stretch for him to move from listening to Delta Blues to Beethoven's Ninth Symphony.

Title Index

First Line Index

CPSIA information can be obtained
at www.ICGtesting.com
Printed in the USA
BVHW071052031122
651060BV00013B/407